KÖNIGSKINDER

KÖNIGSKINDER

(ROYAL CHILDREN)

A GUIDE TO ENGELBERT HUMPERDINCK'S
AND ERNST ROSMER'S OPERA

By
LEWIS M. ISAACS AND KURT J. RAHLSON

ILLUSTRATED

NEW YORK
DODD, MEAD AND COMPANY
1912

Lewis M. Isaacs and Kurt J. Rahlson:

Königskinder
(Royal Children)
A Guide to Engelbert Humperdinck's
and Ernst Rosmer's Opera.

First published by Dodd, Mead & Co 1912.

Republished Travis & Emery 2009.

Published by
Travis & Emery Music Bookshop
17 Cecil Court, London, WC2N 4EZ, United Kingdom.
(+44) 20 7240 2129
neworders@travis-and-emery.com

Hardback: ISBN10: 1-904331-79-3   ISBN13: 978-1904331-79-7
Paperback: ISBN10: 1-904331-80-7   ISBN13: 978-1-904331-80-3

Engelbert Humperdinck (1854-1921). German composer.

He attended Cologne Conservatory (1872-1876) and the Royal Music School in Munich.. He later worked with Wagner in Bayreuth.

His famous works are Hänsel und Gretel (1893), Königskinder (1897) and incidental music for four Shakespeare plays (1907-1908).

More details available from
- Stanley Sadie: The New Grove Dictionary of Music and Musicians.
- http://en.wikipedia.org/wiki/Humperdinck

Very little biographical information available in English.

Travis & Emery are republishing two works by Lewis M. Isaacs and Kurt J. Rahlson - Hänsel and Gretel: A Guide to Humperdinck's Opera and Königskinder (Royal Children): A Guide to Humperdinck's Opera.

DR. ENGELBERT HUMPERDINCK

KÖNIGSKINDER

(ROYAL CHILDREN)

A GUIDE TO ENGELBERT HUMPERDINCK'S
AND ERNST ROSMER'S OPERA

By

LEWIS M. ISAACS AND KURT J. RAHLSON

ILLUSTRATED

NEW YORK
DODD, MEAD AND COMPANY
1912

To

𝔈. 𝔍. ℜ. 𝔍.

(Translated extract from a letter by the composer to the authors.)

STARNBERG, NEAR MUNICH,
September 25, 1911.

Your kind favor was forwarded to me here, at Wurmsee, where I am spending the rest of my vacation. Your " Guide to Königskinder " is being returned, under separate cover, with my best thanks. . . . I have examined it and find it worked out very carefully and with much insight. . . .

With kindest regards and many thanks, I am,

Yours very sincerely,

DR. E. HUMPERDINCK.

PREFACE

Whether Engelbert Humperdinck is in fact the originator of a new genre of opera is of little consequence; since, unquestionably, his essays in the field of "Märchenoper"—or fairy-lore opera—have indissolubly associated his name with it. "Hänsel und Gretel," which scored the greatest operatic success in the latter part of the Nineteenth Century, brought the composer into world-wide prominence; and the spontaneous and charming character of the music has endeared it to every heart. A more striking contrast to the lurid works of the so-called veristic school of Italy, just then in popular vogue, could not be imagined. In place of a crude "raw-head-and-bloody-bones" sort of libretto, there was one of the simple and poetic fairy tales of the brothers Grimm; and the musical setting, so strongly recalling the ever-fresh folksong of Germany, was a most captivating substitute for the raucous, rudely-harmonized—if richly-hued—scores of the prevailing school of opera. It was as though a breath of cool, sweet-smelling air had found its way into the torrid, humid atmosphere that hung heavy over the operatic stage. The choice of subject was, for the composer, a most felicitous one. For Humperdinck

7

is, as the Kaiser has well said, the most Germanic of
living composers. His genius has its roots firmly
embedded in the soil of Germany, with its wonderful
well of folk-song undefiled. The combination of
fairy tale and folk-song, so natural when once sug-
gested, had been attempted by an earlier composer,
who, in his day and ever since, has been called the
most Germanic of operatic composers—Carl Maria
von Weber. Like Humperdinck, Weber utilized
popular melodies in his operas, and his own type of
melody was closely akin to that of the contemporary
Volkslied. His settings of Körner's " Leyer und
Schwert " stimulated national enthusiasm to fever
heat and made him the hero of the day. But Weber
suffered from lack of good librettos, and the per-
vading romantic element had a certain amount of
medievalism and a stilted quality that prevented a
complete balance between music and drama. It
remained for Humperdinck with his strong sense
of the natural beauty of the folk-tune and its kin-
ship to the folk-tale of his native country and with
his individual melodic inventiveness, to recreate
out of elements that were not in themselves new,
an art work which will live through the ages,
refreshing the most blasé music lover and delighting
generations yet unborn. The text, " Lumen de
lumine," from the Nicene Creed, which Humperdinck has placed at the head of his " Königskinder "
score, adds point to the thought that he, like some

runner of old, has kindled his flame at the torch of
Weber and going forward holds it high.

So great a success as " Hänsel und Gretel " won
for itself, it would be difficult to repeat. But in his
latest opera, " Königskinder," the composer has
proven that his musical powers are susceptible of
growth without any loss in spontaneity or freshness.
And if its popular success should be less, it will be
attributable partly to the fact that it followed
" Hänsel und Gretel " and partly to its more seri-
ous, not to say tragic, theme. Once more the composer has utilized a simple fairy tale, only this time
a tale with an underlying symbolical significance
which adds to its dramatic interest. The tragedy of
the wasted lives of the royal children, unwelcomed
because unrecognized, is the tragedy of human folly
and blindness which judges by externals, and fails,
until too late, to appreciate true inward worth. The
story lends itself easily to musical treatment. As in
" Hänsel und Gretel," the composer has modeled
his melody largely on the folk-song pattern, devel-
oping it with marvellous technical skill and all the
resources of the modern orchestra. And the balance
between the drama and the music is preserved with
even better judgment. At no time does one feel
that a trip-hammer is being used to crush an egg-
shell—a sense of incongruity which does at times
obtrude itself in the earlier opera. Unlike " Hänsel
und Gretel," " Königskinder " is built up of a num-

ber of "leit-motive" or typical phrases, such as Wagner used with so much dramatic effect in his music dramas. These motives are for the most part extremely simple and well-chosen to express the dramatic points for which they are intended. They are developed, combined and contrasted skillfully; and every device of contrapuntal resource is drawn upon and utilized in a manner apparently so effortless as to produce the effect of utmost simplicity. There is much subtlety in the treatment of the guiding themes in accordance with the Wagnerian precedent, and, as in Wagner's works, the explanatory power of the music is thereby greatly enhanced and the meaning of the text deepened.

Originally, " Königskinder " was merely a play with musical accompaniment, the spoken dialogue at times assuming the semblance of musical pitch. The experiment was not wholly successful; and the composer wisely re-wrote and added to the score until he had made it into an opera, in which form it had its world première at the Metropolitan Opera House last season, under the supervision of the composer himself.

Humperdinck was born at Siegburg, in the Rhine Province, September 1, 1854. He studied under Ferdinand Hiller at the Cologne Conservatory and while there won the Frankfort Mozart prize. By the aid of this money, he went to Munich, where he placed himself first under Franz Lachner and later under Josef Rheinberger, at the Royal Music School. He then won the Mendelssohn Scholarship of Berlin, and proceeded to Italy to continue his studies. At Naples he became acquainted with Wagner and, at his invitation, assisted him at Bayreuth in the preparations for the first production of " Parsifal." It is interesting to note in this connection that the librettist of " Königskinder," " Ernst Rosmer," is a daughter of Heinrich Porges, the " Blumenvater," as he was affectionately dubbed by Wagner, by reason of his services in preparing the Flower Maidens for this " Parsifal " performance. Again Humperdinck won a prize which enabled him to continue his studies still further; and he traveled once more in Italy, France and Spain, settling for ten years at Barcelona, where he taught musical theory at the Conservatory. In 1887 he returned to Cologne, and from 1890 to 1896 was professor at the Hoch Conservatory in Frankfort, as well as teacher in another musical school and newspaper critic. It was during this period that he composed " Hänsel und Gretel," planned originally, it is said, for the delectation of his sister's children. It's success was immediate and brought the composer to a high pinnacle of popularity. In 1896 the Kaiser conferred upon him the honorary title of Professor, and the following year he removed to Boppard, there to continue his composition and teaching. In 1900 he returned to Berlin, succeeding Max Bruch at the Royal Conservatory, as the head of a " Meister-Klasse " in composition, and a member of the Senate of the Royal " Akademie der Künste." Recently he received the title of Doctor, rarely accorded to musicians by German universities.

Humperdinck is of an extremely retiring disposition, which his fame has only served to accentuate. He is reticent about himself, preferring to let his music speak for him. He is wholly engrossed in his work, enjoying his pedagogic activities almost as well as his creative efforts.

In the following pages an attempt has been made to describe " Königskinder " for the music lover who has not a technical knowledge of music. The guide to the thematic material is simple and intended to be used by the layman, who may easily familiarize himself with the leading motives and thus follow the performance more intelligently. The translations from the original text, especially made for this book, will also serve as guides to the story for those who are not familiar with German. If the result is to add to the general interest in this charming work and so to help entrench it in the minds and hearts of opera-goers, the purpose of the " Guide " will have been achieved.

New York, October, 1911.

LEWIS M. ISAACS
KURT J. RAHLSON

ILLUSTRATIONS

CAST OF CHARACTERS OF FIRST PERFORMANCE ON
ANY STAGE OF

KÖNIGSKINDER

(Metropolitan Opera House, New York City, December 28, 1910.)

THE KING'S SON............Hermann Jadlowker
THE GOOSE-GIRL.............Geraldine Farrar
THE FIDDLER...................Otto Goritz
THE WITCH...................Louise Homer
THE WOODCUTTER..............Adamo Didur
THE BROOMMAKER...............Albert Reiss
TWO CHILDREN...............{ Edna Walter
                          { Lotte Engel
THE SENIOR COUNSELLOR.........Marcel Reiner
THE INNKEEPER.............Antonio Pini-Corsi
THE INNKEEPER'S DAUGHTER..Florence Wickham
THE TAILOR....................Julius Bayer
THE STABLEMAID..............Marie Mattfeld
FIRST GATEKEEPER..............Ernst Maran
SECOND GATEKEEPER..........William Hinshaw
CONDUCTOR, Alfred Hertz

THE OPENING SCENE OF "KÖNIGSKINDER"

KÖNIGSKINDER

(ROYAL CHILDREN)

PART I

THE STORY

NOTE

The first appearance of each theme is marked by the music in the body of the text and the name and number of the theme in the left-hand margin. Every recurrence is noted either in the text, or where the narrative does not permit of it there, in the margin, at the point in the narrative where it appears.

KÖNIGSKINDER

IN a small, sunny glade, surrounded by the wooded hills, in back of which lies the town of Hellabrunn, there once stood a tiny hut where a cruel witch lived and practised her black art. Day after day, a faint blue smoke curled from the crooked chimney of the stove where she mixed her poisoned brews and baked the bread that brought swift death to anyone who ate of it. On the roof, a raven with clipped wings hopped restlessly to and fro, and there, too, squatted a yellow tomcat with eyes that gleamed like the witch's own. But not everything showed so plainly the influence of the evil spell that hovered over the place. Near the house there was a little vegetable garden with one tall lily ready to break into flower, and beyond that a fountain, whose clear waters, dripping through the crevices in a mossy tree trunk that served as a trough, formed a tiny pool where twelve wild geese splashed contentedly about. To and from the garden they ran, led by their waddling gray captain, cackling, smoothing their feathers, pulling bits of grass, busily unmindful of everything but their own company, forgetting even the beautiful Goose-Girl who lay nearby on a grassy knoll, well in the shade of an old, old linden-tree.

She had forgotten them, too, as she lay, singing to the rhythm of the running waters and the dancing sunshine. She was dreaming of the world of men and women in the city below, which she could never hope to see while the witch held her bound by the spell of her magic art. Dimly she could remember the day when the crone, whom she believed to be her grandmother, had taken her from the world and brought her to this place. Where she had come from, or why, she did not know. For then she was still too small to lift the door-latch; and, although she had grown year by year, until the waters of the fountain, which she used as a mirror, told her that she had come to beautiful womanhood, the spell was as strong as ever upon her. When she tried to run away, the bushes caught and held her and the hot earth burned her feet at every step. So now she did not try any more, but lived as happily as she could, tending her flowers and her geese, gathering the woodside posies and weaving them into pretty garlands and then lying down to dream in the shade of the old, old linden-tree.

But on the day of which our story tells, as on so many other days, the cruel witch broke in upon her dreams, coming with powders and bitter herbs, and making the Goose-Girl help to knead the pasty, which never grew old or stale, nor lost its evil power. In vain, the maiden breathed a blessing over the loaf:

" Who eats of this shall a vision see,
And true his fairest dream shall be."

The witch's incantation was stronger than anything she could say; and, muttering, " Who eats of
this shall die," the old woman carried the finished
loaf into the hut and hid it in a chest, and then de-
parted into the woods again to gather snails and
worms and gray-green lizards born in the mists of
midnight.

The sound of the witch's footsteps had barely
died away, when the Goose-Girl heard the crackling
of the underbrush behind her, and then a man's
voice, saying, " Good-day, fair Goose-Queen."
Startled, she turned and faced the King's Son. But
she had never seen a man, and could not guess who
this one was. Wearied of idleness and luxury and
golden chains, the King's Son had left his kingdom
in search of freedom, leaving behind him, too, his
royal robes and everything that hinted at the
grandeur of the court. He was dressed as a hunts-
man, with his cross-bow and quiver and a bundle
slung over his shoulder. He was a slender youth,
pale, with flashing eyes and royal mien, which he
could not doff as he could the badges of his rank.
And the Goose-Girl looked at him and loved him;
and the King's Son looked at the beautiful Goose-
Girl and loved her, too. Together, they sat down
under the linden-tree and talked of love and life,

of Kings and their courts, of Goose-Girls and
their flocks. And when a gust of wind blew off the
maiden's wreath of flowers, the King's Son picked
it up as some dear treasure, and, opening his bundle,
took out the crown which was hidden there and
offered it to the Goose-Girl in exchange. But the
crown was only gold and meaningless to her, and
she would not take it. So the King's Son threw it
away and, rising, offered her himself, begging her
to go forth into the world with him.

Eagerly she consented, and, hand in hand, they
started out in search of freedom. But she had forgotten the magic spell. A heavy wind shook the
trees; the cat put up his back; the raven croaked;
the geese, frightened into silence, huddled around
the maiden, who stood rooted to the spot, unable
to go another step. Then the King's Son, who did
not understand the power that held the Goose-Girl,
cried out against her cowardice, and, turning dis-
dainfully away, sallied forth alone, angrily protest-
ing that she should never see him again until a star
from heaven pierced the blossom of her lily.

The Goose-Girl threw herself upon the ground,
sobbing bitterly and crying out against the fate that
had not made her, too, a royal child. But there was
not much time for sorrowing and tears, for the old
witch was calling from the woods. The Goose-Girl
remembered the crown which the King's Son had
thrown away, and, fearing that the witch would

steal it, she quickly called the old gray goose to her, and, giving her the crown, ordered her to hide it; and the sly old goose carried it into the shrubbery and concealed it there. The Goose-Girl still showed only too plainly the effects of her encounter, when the witch returned.

"Why do you hold your hand to your head, hussy?" asked the crone; "and why are your cheeks so pale?"

"I have just bathed them in cool water," answered the maiden.

"Why is your mouth as red as blood?"

"From the red berries I have eaten," answered the maiden.

The witch threw down her bundle and put her hand on the girl's heart.

"Why," she asked, "do your heart-beats falter so?"

Then, in her great fear, the Goose-Girl answered: "Oh, Grandmother, I have seen a man."

At first the witch refused to believe that such a thing was possible and thought the Goose-Girl had been dreaming. When she found out that it was the truth, her anger knew no bounds, and, threatening the direst punishments, she pushed the Goose-Girl into the hut and swore that she should remain locked in forever, so that she might never see a man again. But before the door had closed upon her, the maiden heard the sound of singing in the woods. Nearer and nearer came the voice, and soon three men stood before the hut, calling loudly to the witch.

They were three citizens of Hellabrunn, the Fiddler, the Woodcutter and the Broommaker. They had been sent to the witch, whom the people believed to be the wise woman of the Woods, to ask her to name a king for their village, weary of the freedom it had had since the death of the old King. At first the witch refused to believe that there could be people so foolish as to long for chains, but when the ambassadors persisted, she said to them:

> " Go, this word to your fellows bringing,
> To-morrow, when noonday bells are ringing,
> And all, for the feast of Hella arrayed,
> Are gathered together in mead and glade,
> The first who saunters into your town,
> Though a changeling he, or a rogue, may be,
> He shall wear your crown."

The Broommaker and the Woodcutter, who were sordid men, went gaily off, homeward bound; for they had been promised large sums of gold if their mission was sucessfully fulfilled. But the Fiddler lingered. As they talked, he had seen the Goose-Girl through the open casement, and he knew there was some mystery about her. His spirit was above dross, and he was glad enough to be parted from his unworthy fellows. Cunningly, he forced the witch to let the girl come out to him; and soon

he knew the whole story of her meeting with the
King's Son and of how their love for each other had
been thwarted by the enchantment which had held
her all her life. To the Fiddler, the beautiful girl
herself seemed royal, and so he told the witch. But
the old crone jeered at such pretensions. The girl,
she said, was a child of shame, murder her heritage,
sin her only crown. And her parents were no royal
pair, but the hangman's daughter and his apprentice,
whose death-watch was their wedding night. Still,
maintained the gentle Fiddler, true royalty was
of the soul alone, and if the ill-starred parents
had loved royally and made the noblest sacrifice
for love, the girl, their child, was royal still, and it
remained with her to break the chains that bound
her and kept her from the realm which was hers
by right. His words gave the Goose-Girl new hope
and the fresh strength bred of hope. Taking the
crown in both her hands, she prayed fervently for
help, imploring the spirits of her father and mother
to send some sign to guide her in the way of right.
As she prayed, a star from heaven fell into the heart
of her lily, and she remembered the parting words
of the King's Son, and rose joyously, feeling the
burden of the spell depart from her and knowing
she was free. With the good Fiddler as her companion, she left the haunted glade, not heeding the
witch's imprecations, eager only to find the King's
Son, whom she loved.

The King's Son meanwhile had wandered for-
lornly on, until he came to the town of Hellabrunn,
where, for want of a better resting-place, he lay
down with the swine to sleep. Even there the vision
of the beautiful Goose-Girl followed him and made
sleep pleasant; although when he awoke, his dream
was gone from him, and only a blurred memory
remained to trouble him. By the time he went to
the tavern in search of work, the whole town was
astir. The Broommaker and the Woodcutter had
returned from their journey, with wild, forged tales
of the horrors they had undergone from desperate
monsters in the enchanted woods. They were the
heroes of the hour. The witch, they said, had promised them that at the stroke of twelve the King
would appear within the city gates. The day had
been proclaimed a city festival; and in the public
square, outside the tavern and facing the city gates,
everyone was busily employed scrubbing, dusting,
cooking, watering the wine, all in preparation for
the jubilee. The waitresses and the Innkeeper's
Daughter found time to coquette with the comely
youth who came so sadly, yet with such dignity; but
the King's Son scorned them all. Everything re-
minded him of the beautiful maiden whose wreath
he still cherished. The power of the forgotten dream
grew stronger upon him as the morning wore on and
as the crowd assembled, dancing, singing, gaily waiting for the royal claimant who was to come. Just

as the noonday bells began to strike, the picture of his dream came back to him. It was not a king he saw, as the people expected, riding up in regal state and royally attended, but his own lovely Goose-Girl, with her geese for retinue and the crown of the King's Son upon her head. And so it happened. At the stroke of twelve the merrymaking ceased; even the Broommaker's thirteen children stopped their happy frolic while the gates were opened in expectant silence.

And there she stood, the Goose-Girl, royally beautiful and good, with the crown of the King's Son upon her head and the light of noonday surrounding her like a halo. Her geese were behind her, and beside her stood the gentle Fiddler, her sole guide and companion. When she saw the King's Son, she entered the gates and hastened to him, and he proudly proclaimed her Queen. But the indignant villagers scorned the thought of a queen in rags. Angrily they spurned her, thrusting both the Royal Children out of their gates with jeers and curses, and casting the Fiddler into prison for what they considered his wicked hoax. Only a little child, who had played with the King's Son and who saw things with the clear, true eyes of youth, was left in the square, so lately full of gaiety, mourning the Royal Children.

For a long time after this unhappy day, the villagers could think of nothing else than of how to punish all those concerned in their disappointment. The old witch was burned at the stake; the Broommaker and the Woodcutter were condemned to public obloquy. But saddest of all was the fate of the poor, faithful Fiddler. Weary months he languished in prison, with no one to lighten the gloom except the one sweet child who had recognized the Royal Children and knew him for their friend. And when at last the prison gates were opened, his cruel jailers lamed the gentle man before they set him free. But his heart was too full of sorrow for the lost Children to find room for pity for himself; and with his fiddle for company, he set out in search of them. Straight back through the woods he hastened, taking the beaten track to the old witch's hut, hoping that the Goose-Girl might have found her way back to the only place she had ever called her home. But they were not there; and so he made himself a bed in the hut and rested. And every day he took a different road over the hills and through the forest, searching, but all in vain.

Summer had gone and winter had come to take its place; and still there was no sign of the sweet Goose-Girl and her kingly lover. So, in the long winter evenings, the Fiddler wound himself a bier of evergreen twigs and waited to die, since life was not worth living if the Children could not be found. One cold, cold day, when the wind was blowing and snow covered the ground, the children of the town

of Hellabrunn, with the Broommaker and the
Woodcutter as their guides, came to the cabin and
begged the Fiddler to return to them, saying that
Hellabrunn was sad without his music. Their plead-
ings could not shake his purpose; but he loved the
children and took them with him on his search, leaving the sordid men waiting in the cabin.

And there on the hillside, just as the sound of
the fiddle and of the singing had died away, the
Royal Children appeared, weak and weary almost
unto death. All these months they had been seeking
the path homeward to the lost kingdom, straying
from hill to hill, sleeping in caves and forests, eat-
ing what they could shoot or find, until the last
arrow was lost and the last berry frozen. Yet the
dignity of their spirit remained unbroken and the
splendor of their love undimmed.

There was a moment's gladness as the Goose-
Girl recognized the glade, with the familiar hut,
the fountain and the dear old linden-tree, in whose
shade they had sat so happily that day in the spring.
The King's Son ran to the hut, and knocking at
the door, begged for food. But the Woodcutter
did not recognize him, and was too heartless to give
to the hungry without reward; so the youth returned, empty-handed and sorrowful, to his fainting
love. But she for whom he suffered would not
admit her hunger or her pain. Springing up, she
threw aside her mantle, took off her slippers, and,

with a song upon her lips, danced before her lover—
danced until the struggling spirit failed her and she
fell fainting on the snow-covered ground. Then the
King's Son, casting about in his despair, remembered the crown which he carried in his bundle, and,
breaking it in two, he knocked again at the cabin
door and offered gold for bread. And the Woodcutter and his companion, ever greedy, tempted by
the glittering metal, searched in every corner of
the hut, until at last they came upon the chest where
the witch, so long ago, had hidden the poisoned
bread. And this they traded for the crown.

As though it were a feast, happily, gaily, the
King's Son bore his prize to the fair Goose-Girl,
and, dividing it into two equal parts, they ate it
bit by bit. Quickly the cruel magic worked; but
the blessing which the Goose-Girl had breathed over
the loaf was not without its power. "Who eats
of this," she had prayed, "shall a vision see ";
and so it was dreaming of roses and of summertime
that they died together, there on the hillside, under
the linden-tree.

And when the Fiddler and his train came back
again, they found them—the lost Royal Children.
And they lifted them on to the bier of evergreen
boughs, which the Fiddler had made against his
own death; and, singing, the children and the Fiddler bore them to a royal grave.

KÖNIGSKINDER
(ROYAL CHILDREN)

PART II

THE MUSIC

THE GOOSE-GIRL FEEDING HER FLOCK

Prelude to Act I

Far away in his kingdom beyond the
mountains, the King's Son, athirst for
happiness, threw off his golden chains
and started out into the world alone to
search for it. With his going there began the story of the " Royal Children."
So the composer, as a fitting introduction to the tale, gives us a picture of the
King's Son in the Prelude, that and little
else, written in E Flat, which is to be his
distinguishing key. The Prelude opens
with the motive of the King's Son in
Quest (1) of happiness, a horn call,
full of the spirit of brave adventure in
which he leaves his home.

Quest (1)

It is the final phrase of this motive
that gives it its special meaning, distinguishing it from the King's Son (2),
which, instead of taking the downward
turn of the Quest (1), moves steadily

33

on and upward, like one to whom the heavens are more real than earth.

**King's
Son (2)**

The final phrase of the QUEST (1), on the other hand, itself becomes significant, apart from the rest of the motive, in the early passages of the love scene. It is, in fact, the root of all the love music, since, with the same descending sequence, but with a greater interval which makes it deeper and richer in feeling, it dominates the love music throughout the opera, filling, as it were, the role of a LOVE MOTTO (20).

**Love
Motto (20)**

Although, before the Prelude ends, we have the LOVE MOTTO (20) alone, emphasizing its importance in the drama that is to follow, it appears first as an integral part of the winsome motive of FLIRTATION (4).

Flirtation (4)

Besides these motives, all derived
from or related to the QUEST (1), the
Prelude introduces two others—the
DIVINE DISCONTENT (3), which later
becomes a familiar accompaniment to
the story in which the striving for the
unattainable plays so large a part,

Divine Dis-
content (3)

and the figure, almost at the close, beginning in the bass and borne upward
by the violoncello, which breathes of
LONGING (5), and which appears again,
slightly altered, characterizing the first
scene between the King's Son and the
Goose-Girl.

Longing (5)

Act I

As though to imply that it was the
might of their LONGING (5) that
brought them together, this motive
drops quickly from E Flat to G Major,
which is the Goose-Girl's key; and as
the curtain lifts, we have, in that key,
the simple but graphic motive of the
LINDEN (6) under which the Goose-
Girl is lying, singing and dreaming.

Linden (6)

All through the fairy-lore of Germany, the linden has been associated
with whatever is most romantic and
fanciful; and it is suggestive that again
and again in " Königskinder " it is the
Goose-Girl's motive, and not that of
the tree itself, which accompanies the
mention of the linden in the text. **In**

this first instance, the LINDEN (6) directly precedes the equally simple and graceful motive of the GOOSE-GIRL (7).

Goose-Girl (7)

Thematically and psychologically, this motive is so closely allied to that of the KING's SON (2) and to the one, later to be developed, of the ROYAL CHILDREN (8), as to suggest strongly the spiritual alliance between the characters.

Royal Children (8)

All three fall into the compass of an octave, each beginning at the lowest note and ascending to the highest, yet with rhythmic variations that leave the characters as definitely distinguished as they are closely related.

The SPINDLE SONG (9) which the Goose-Girl is humming, while not, strictly speaking, a motive, appears several times in the opera as a symbol, and should be noted.

Spindle Song (9)

And the Geese! Ah, they are a part
of the story. Here, when the Goose-
Girl calls her flock to order, we have
the first appearance of their motive
—a dissonance repeated in rapid succession—combined with that of the KING'S
SON (2), and are given a hint of the
allegory which is to come:

Geese (10)

You sit on the hillock,
He sits on his throne.
As you the geese,
So he his people guards.

(Du sitz'st auf dem Hügel,
Er sitzt auf dem Thron.
Gänse musst du,
Er muss Menschen hüten.)

The Witch is the first of the characters to speak, yet she comes and goes
without a theme. Nor does she have
one in the whole scene in which she plays
so large a part; for it is not the Witch
herself who influences the destinies of
the Royal Children, but the WITCHERY
OF NATURE (11) perverted to her
uses. To her

How fine the nights,
When on moonlit heights,
With poisonous milks the grasses
   swell.

(Die Nacht ist schön,
Wenn auf mondbleichen Höh'n
Von giftiger Milch die Kräuter
   schwellen.)

Witchery of
Nature (11)

Nature, so viewed, is abhorrent to
the Goose-Girl, who runs from it to
her tiny garden with its one budding
flower. And there we hear the motive
of the lily, the symbol of purity, a theme
which, with slight development, is hereafter always used **to symbolize** the
Goose-Girl's own PURITY (12).

Purity (12)

It indicates, in a way, her beauty of
character, just as the theme next heard,

when she recalls how she looked in
the fountain, represents her physical
BEAUTY (13).

Beauty (13)

Inversion
of (7).

In this, the composer neatly illustrates
the way in which an extra-musical idea
can be translated into music; for the
BEAUTY mirrored in the fountain is an
exact inversion of the GOOSE-GIRL'S
(7) own theme.

The struggle, musical as well as
spiritual, between the Goose-Girl and
the world of magic in which she lives,
has but begun; and when the old crone
returns, breaking in upon the girl's
memories of her childhood (cf. No. 48)
with complaints of carelessness and in-
attention to the rules of witchery, the
theme of WITCHCRAFT (14) which
accompanies her tirade is in strong contrast to the music which preceded it.

**Witchcraft
(14)**

This WITCHCRAFT (14) is a strange
harmonic progression which makes a
fitting frame for the motive of the
POISONED LOAF (15), which appears
in outline as the flour is dampened and
the dough is kneaded.

**Poisoned
Loaf (15)**

The Goose-Girl knows only too well
that the wicked work must go on, and
that she must fulfill her part of it; but
this only serves to remind her more
forcibly of her utter disharmony with
her surroundings. So far, all the music
that depicts the girl has been simple,
beautiful, pure—as her Creator made
her; here, for the first time, we get a
glimpse of the girl's soul, tormented by
the conditions under which she lives.
For want of a better name, we call this
DISTRESS (16); but reappearing again

Distress (16)

and again, the motive is made to repre-
sent many different emotions, always

with an inner sense of the spiritual con-
flict with material things, the effect upon
the girl's consciousness of the magic all
about, and especially of the SPELL (17)
that holds her fast. The music of the
SPELL (17)—" Enchanted every tree
and shrub; they'll hold you fast " (Im
Zuber stehen Baum und Strauch. Die

Spell (17)

halten dich)—stands logically between
the first statement of the girl's DIS-
TRESS (16) and its working out as the
girl openly bewails her misery.

" Oh, how great a woe is mine!
Who cannot what I would,
And would not what I can."

'(Ach, was ist mir solche Not!
Kann nicht, was ich mag!
Mag nicht, was ich kann!)

And as the work is finished and the
phrase ends " Here is the bread," the
musical idea, too, is completed by the
full motive of the POISONED LOAF

(15), which is further turned and developed by the Witch until out of it grows prophetically the motive of DEATH (18).

" 'Twill never redden a cheek again.
In a secret chest I will bury it safe."

Death (18)

When the loaf has been safely stowed away, the witch comes from the hut with the basket in which she gathers snails and roots and powders; and as she goes into the woods, gloating over the red mist that fell at midnight, the music of the WITCHERY OF NATURE (11) gradually dies away. So, too, the Goose-Girl's unhappiness, and almost before the old crone is out of hearing, we listen to the SPINDLE SONG (9) again, bringing back the mood in which the story opened.

There follows one of the gayest passages in the opera. The Goose-Girl, care-free again, dives into her pocket and throws crumbs to her flock; then, bedecking herself, goes merrily and impulsively to her fountain mirror, and, as

Geese (10)

she looks in, calls to her geese to see
her. "How fair am I" (Ei, bin ich
schön), she sings, and the geese seem to
echo the sentiment. In this passage, in
such quick succession as fairly to over-
lap, we have the motive of the GEESE
(10), a new one to characterize her
girlish IMPULSIVENESS (19), GOOSE-
GIRL (7), BEAUTY (13), and, once
more, the GEESE (10).

Impulsive-
ness (19)

Then the Goose-Girl hears the crackling boughs, and sighs as she thinks it is
her grandmother returning all too soon.
But we know better, for even before we
see him or hear his "Good-day, fair
Goose-Queen," the music tells us that it
is the King's Son on his QUEST (1) for
happiness.

The scene between the King's Son
and the Goose-Girl is marked by a
swift and steady emotional crescendo.
The musical basis of the whole scene is
the last phrase of the QUEST (1), appearing still in the original form when
the King's Son asks, "Have you no

greeting for a simple wayfarer?"
(Hast keinen freundsamen Gruss einem
schlichten Wandersmann?), but chang-
ing as he looks at her, and the object of
his quest defines itself—for us, at first,
rather than for him—into the LOVE
MOTTO (20), which, as noted in the
Prelude, forms a part of FLIRTATION
(4) in the line, "Maiden, your lips are
red as a rose" (Mägdlein, wie hast du
so roten Mund).

Question and answer develop this
FLIRTATION (4) motive into a melodi-
ous episode, which we leave only when
we arrive, in the course of the narrative,
at a new series of themes descriptive of
the life of the King's Son before his
quest began. The first to appear, answers the maiden's query, "Is that a
sword?" (Ist das ein Schwert?) and
received, in conjunction with the lines,

"You've guessed aright.
Of little worth;
It has, as yet, no name."
(Geraten gut.
Nicht viel wert.
Noch hat's keinen Namen.)

it brings to mind NOTHUNG, the sword
most familiar to music-lovers, besides

which the SWORD of the King's Son is, as the theme hints, a mere toy.

Sword (21)

(Nothung)

The Goose-Girl, however, with the quick insight born of love, sees that there is valor in the man, which will soon temper the steel; and we hear the SWORD (21) motive combined with one which marks the King's Son as the heir of a royal race.

Royalty (22)

Purity (12)

As she studies him, he watches her, too. Suddenly, the full appreciation of her spirituality comes to him and is heightened by the lightheartedness with which she goes to draw water for him from the well. Then for him, too, the vision clears, and he knows that it is no mysterious something he is seeking, but this LOVE (20) which he has found, though not yet realized. Gradually, the GOOSE-GIRL'S (7) own theme is en-

Impulsive-ness (19)

Quest (1)

Longing (5)

twined with his LONGING (5); and so
the love music is left, while the King's
Son takes up once more the story of his

Quest (1)

life. The music marks his memories
not only of the royal line from whom he

Royalty (22)

is descended, but of the REGAL STATE
(23) in which they lived in the kingdom far back of the mountains.

**Regal
State (23)**

" There," he concludes, " I stood in the
service of the King." (Da bin ich in
Diensten dem König gestanden.)

And this introduces the motive of the
YOUNG PRINCE (24), a theme obvi-
ously derived from ROYALTY (22), yet
as simple and graceful as that of the
GOOSE-GIRL (7), and, significantly
enough, in her characteristic key (G
Major).

**Young
Prince (24)**

Here the theme is used to depict the
Young Prince in his relation to the
duties which forge his connection, as it

were, with the royalty which he has just described.

To stand in the service of a King, however, means little to the Goose-Girl, who has no idea what a king may be. It is while the King's Son is puzzling out the simplest way to explain these things that he hits upon the analogy, already quoted, between the Goose-Girl sitting upon her hillock, guarding her flock, and the King upon his throne, ruling his subjects. Gradually, as her mind grasps the idea, the music drops the combination of the GEESE (10) and KING'S SON (2) motives, develops the KING'S SON (2) alone, and rises from that to a solemn, unadorned presentation of ROYALTY (22) at the lines which give the ideal of kingship:

Geese (10) and King's Son (2)

" And if his task he rightly knows,
And blamelessly through life he
goes,
From every prayer a blessing
flows."

(Und wenn er's so recht versteht
Und herzenshell über die Erde
geht
Dann segnet er alles mit seinem
Gebet.)

Continuing, he recounts to her the
things that distinguish the heir-apparent
from the king; and here the motive of
the YOUNG PRINCE (24) typifies the
golden cradle in which he sleeps, the
wonderful raiment he wears, his grace,
his innocence, his powers, his privileges
—anything that added to the experience
of the Young Prince helped to breed in
his soul that yearning for a life without
Divine Dis- gold and golden chains, which made a
content (3) wanderer of him.

" Out! Away!
  At the dawn of day
  He flees the sleep of the palace
      walls."

(Fort! Hinaus!
  In der Morgenhelle
  Entflieht er dem schlafenden Kö-
      nigshaus.)

But when he left, he was no longer
Royalty (22) the Young Prince. The royal blood
within him was awake; and aspiration,
the DIVINE DISCONTENT (3), above
all, the struggle with the hard realities
of Nature, soon made of him the true
King's Son.

" King's Son,
  The true King's Son,
  Can you follow the words of the
      fool?"

(Königskind,
  Echtes Königskind!
  Kannst du den Narren verstehn?)

So he ends. And for all answer the Goose-Girl says, "I would go with him." (Möcht' mit ihm gehn.)

How well she understands, the music tells better than her words, by the change of key from E flat to G Major and then their constant interchange, by the apposition of the motives of the YOUNG PRINCE (24) and the GOOSE-GIRL (7), "King and Beggarmaid" (König und Bettlerin), above all by the Goose-Girl's adoption of the DIVINE DISCONTENT (3), which had been his guide to true royalty.

The WOOING (25) which follows, begins with the song of the King's Son, "Will you my Maytime Sweetheart be, you fairest flower?" (Willst du mein Maienbuhle sein, du Blumenweiche?),

Wooing (25)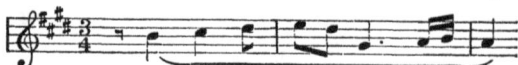

THE FIDDLER

which contains, besides the LOVE
MOTTO (20) and the theme of the
GOOSE-GIRL (7)—used, it should be
noted, when he speaks of the linden-
tree—the motive of their new CON-
TENTMENT (26).

Contentment
(26)

The musical succession in the episode
is as quick and flowing as it is full of
suggestion. When the King's Son begs
for a kiss, he does it with a plea of the
joy and CONTENTMENT (26) it would
bring; as their lips meet and they sit
close to each other in quiet peace, there
is a welding of the DIVINE DISCON-
TENT (3), the LOVE MOTTO (20), the
GOOSE-GIRL (7), YOUNG PRINCE (24)
and the final CONTENTMENT (26).
The psychology of the sequence is
simple.

Equally simple, too, the quick disharmony when a gust of wind, with a recall
of the WITCHERY OF NATURE (11),
blows off the Goose-Girl's wreath, and
it is torn in her effort to regain it from
Distress (16) the King's Son. The wreath itself has
had no motive; the TORN WREATH

(27), however, with its added symbolic
significance, is given one.

**Torn Wreath
(27)**

Following this closely, comes the motive of the CROWN (28), which the
King's Son takes from his bundle and
offers to the Goose-Girl in exchange for
the wreath. Like the motive of the
YOUNG PRINCE (24), this is clearly related to that of ROYALTY (22).

Crown (28)

From this point, the love scene contains nothing musically new, both voice
and orchestra carrying constant reminis-
cences of the LOVE MOTTO (20),
SWORD (21), YOUNG PRINCE (24)
and CROWN (28) motives, until the
SPELL (17) reappears when the maiden
tries to run away with the King's Son,
and cannot. Then it is more than reminiscence; it is repeated contrast, com-

bination, opposition—the SPELL (17)
and DISTRESS (16), BEAUTY (13) and
DISTRESS (16), YOUNG PRINCE (24)
and GOOSE-GIRL (7), SPELL (17),
QUEST (1) and LOVE MOTTO (20) in
the minor—all marking the Goose-
Girl's double struggle, with the forces
of Nature which will not set her free,
and with the King's Son who does not,
cannot understand. At last he has
gone, alone. Her sense of the SPELL
(17) and the LOVE (20) so strangely
interwoven in her destiny are all that
are left to her as she falls, sobbing, to
the earth; and the motive of BEAUTY
(13) is blunted to a minor, and that of
DISTRESS (16) is darkened to despair.

" Go, you have robbed me of my
        love!
Sun, grow blind!
Woods, grow bare!
I'll crush every bloom in the mead-
        ows there
If he does not return.
Oh, Wind, Wind, Wind,
Were I but born of royal kind."

(Geht! Ihr habt ihn mir genommen.
Sonne, werde blind!

Wald, werde grau!
Alle Blumen zerreiss' ich auf
    der Au'
Wird er nicht wiederkommen.
Wind! Wind! Wind!
Wär ich doch auch ein Königs-
    kind.)

Purity (12)

The witch returns, adding her presence to the terrors of the moment; but
the scene between her and the Goose-
Girl is thematically unimportant. As
it is ending, the witch vows that she will
keep the girl out of the sight of men
hereafter, even though it be necessary

Spell (17)
Distress (16)

to lock her in the hut and bind her
anew with a three-fold curse. Just then,
in the distance is heard the jolly and all-
too-brief song of the Fiddler, "Three
fools set forth one day" (Drei Narren
zogen aus), closing with the refrain

"Hei, hei, Tandaradei,"

which possesses a musical significance of
its own, heightened by a slight though
hardly fanciful resemblance to the motive of REGAL STATE (23).

**Tandaradei
(29)**

Hei!   Hei!   Tan - da - ra - dei!

This, with its development and a
reminiscence of the WITCHCRAFT (14),
as the witch pushes the Goose-Girl into
the hut, form a quick transition to a
mood as different from that of the love
scene as was that from the one which
preceded it.

With the first strains of the AMBAS-
SADORS (30) motive,

" Forward, Brother Woodcutter,
Forward, Brother Broommaker,"

(Vorwärts, Bruder Holzhacker,
Vorwärts, Bruder Besenbinder),

we are on earth, our feet firmly planted
in the clay.

Ambassadors
(30)

Only the Fiddler remains out of the
picture; and what his companions think
of their " unruly comrade and his fid-
dling " (der liederliche Genoss, mit
seinem Geigenspiel) is expressly set
forth in the music with which they an-
notate their comments, a theme called

THE FIDDLER AS ROGUE (31), and
which must not be confused with the
one, to appear a little later, of the Fiddler as he really is.

**Fiddler as
Rogue (31)**

The Broommaker diplomatically begins negotiations with the witch by
asking, "My good wife, won't you buy
a broom?" (Gute Frau, kauft ihr
keinen Besen?); and the composer em-
phasizes the humor of the situation by
introducing the theme of the WITCH'S
RIDE, from "Hänsel und Gretel."

**Witch's Ride
(32)**

It will be remembered that the witch
has no motive of her own, because she is
not conceived as personally influencing
the story of the ROYAL CHILDREN. So,

too, with the citizens of Hellabrunn.
Neither the Broommaker nor the
Woodcutter has a theme apart from
the one which represents them jointly
as Ambassadors; while the FIDDLER's
(33) personality is distinguished from
the rest as soon as he jests with the
witch about the flame her wonderful red
eyes have kindled in his heart. His motive, a sprightly violin strain, appears
coupled and contrasted with the AM-
BASSADORS (30).

Fiddler (33)

It is to the Fiddler that most of the
interest in this scene attaches. It is he
who describes to the witch the conditions in Hellabrunn which make the people weary of their freedom and anxious
to have a king again. As he speaks, the
Goose-Girl comes, unnoticed, to the
window and hears the FIDDLER (33)
tell of the throne which they are ready
to build for the scion of a royal house.
His words awaken memories of what
her lover had told her of his history;

Regal State
(23)

Purity (12)
and
Royalty (22)

and we hear a snatch of the SWORD
(21) motive and a repetition of the
REGAL STATE (23).

Just then the Fiddler catches sight of
the Goose-Girl, and the musical delinea-
tion of what occurs is of more than
usual subtlety and brilliance. Unlike the
King's Son, the Fiddler hardly notices
the maiden's beauty. It is the lovely

Purity (12)

soul shining through her eyes that
strikes him at the first glance, and his
own soul rises to meet it. The Fiddler's
motive, ennobled—FIDDLER AS APOSTLE

Royalty (22)

(34)—starts and stops abruptly, giving
way to the AMBASSADORS (30) as he
realizes suddenly the possibility that
here is the royal scion they are seeking.

**Fiddler as
Apostle (34)**

**Fiddler as
Rogue (31)**

His long speech ends with a jest;
and neither the witch nor the other citizens know anything of what has happened. Impatient of them, one and all,
the witch makes her prophecy that to-
morrow's noonday bells will usher in

their king. Here for the first time appears the motive of the ROYAL CHILDREN (8) already noted because of its close relation to those of the KING'S SON (2) and the GOOSE-GIRL (7).

Their mission accomplished, the Woodcutter and Broommaker are eager to go home to receive their promised wage. The one thing that mars their glee is the thought that a third—the Fiddler, who has intruded himself—must share with them. The **Fiddler as Rogue (31)** Fiddler, on the other hand, is anxious to be alone with the witch, to solve the mystery of the beautiful girl whom he has seen. So he tells the citizens he does not want their gold, chases them out into the woods and comes back, **Ambassadors (30)** whistling his favorite air, "TANDARA-DEI" (29). The FIDDLER (33) persuades the witch to let the GOOSE-GIRL **Purity (12)** (7) come out; and as she tells him her story the music weaves a wonderful web of the motives of the SPELL (17), the QUEST (1), PURITY (12) and the LOVE MOTTO (20). The Fiddler understands her tale almost better than she does herself,

" You shall wed the son of the King,"
(Dem Königssohn wirst du dich ver-
    mählen),

he says, and the music carries on the
FIDDLER'S (33) theme beside that of
PURITY (12) and of the QUEST (1).
Again his deeper understanding is em-
phasized when he recognizes that the
hangman's daughter and his apprentice
earned their title to ROYALTY (22) by
the majesty of their love and their
suffering.

The climax of the act is reached
when the Goose-Girl, through the power
of her will, achieves her own freedom.
The musical setting is a symphonic development of much of the material
which has gone before, with recurring
emphasis on the SPELL (17), ROYALTY
(22), GOOSE-GIRL (7) and FIDDLER
(33). When the Goose-Girl prays to
her father and mother for help, ROY-
ALTY (22) appears, simple, complete
and majestic; and a moment later the
Tandaradei curtain falls, as, singing, the FIDDLER
(29) (33) and the Goose-Girl go on their
way out of the enchanted woods, together.

INTRODUCTION TO ACT II

As the first act was called " The King's Son," so the second is " The Hellafestival "; but the introduction, instead of being like the first, a reminiscent narrative, is a simple presentment of what is taking place in the village of Hellabrunn on the day appointed as the festival of the King. The opening phrase is the theme of the FESTIVAL (35).

Festival (35)

It is gay, almost to hilarity, and with a certain jubilance which marks it as the note of a special feast day and a thing apart from the FOLK-DANCE (36) which follows it,

Folk-Dance (36)

just as that is marked by its staider
form from the " RING-A-ROSY " (37),

Ring-a-Rosy
(37)

to which the children are frolicking.
These three motives complete the thematic material of the introduction.

ACT II

As the curtain rises, a new DANCE
MELODY (38) is heard in the distance.

Dance
Melody (38)

The suggestion, so far, is all of the
festive spirit of the day; but the theme
which accompanies the opening words
of the Stablemaid makes the BOUR-
GEOISIE (39) of the people apparent at
once.

Bourgeoisie
(39)

When the Stablemaid says to the
Innkeeper's Daughter,

" You yourself, I suppose, will wel-
come His Majesty,"

[(Ihr werdet wohl selbst den König
empfangen)

she sings the motive of COQUETRY (40)
which, with the BOURGEOISIE (39),
forms the foundation upon which this
scene is built, appearing even when the
King's Son laughingly takes up their
declaration of honor due to royalty.

" The King himself would not pre-
sume to believe it "

(Das vermisst sich der König selbst
nicht zu glauben.)

Coquetry (40)

Ihr wer-det wohl selbst den Kö-nig em - pfan- gen?

Only once is the spirit of the incident
interrupted to let the violoncello sound
the motive of the ROYAL CHILDREN
(8), when the King's Son speaks of the
mystic dream whose content he has forgotten, though the impress is still upon
him. Then it runs frivolously on
again, until the INNKEEPER'S DAUGH-
TER (41) offers the King's Son food

and wine, and, as though by assuming
her duties as hostess, achieves a motive
of her own, which is reiterated when-
ever she is spoken of in this capacity,
and seldom otherwise.

Innkeeper's Daughter (41)

It is not long before the atmosphere
of the scene becomes distasteful to the
King's Son; and it needs only the fra-
grance of the tree under which he is sitting to bring back the memories of the

Linden (6)

day before. The sneer of the INN-
KEEPER'S DAUGHTER (41) only serves
to emphasize the difference; and when
the odor of the LINDEN (6) suggests
the mystic dream again, the frivolity
ceases, and the music travels with the
thoughts of the King's Son, gathering
one more slight clue to the dream.

Goose-Girl (7)

Goose-Girl (7)

Now the idea of the GOOSE-GIRL (7)
is insistently opposed to that of the INN-
KEEPER'S DAUGHTER (41); and her
COQUETRY (40) draws from him only
the words,

Royal Children (8)

Love Motto (20)

" Oh, my lovely Goose-Girl "

(O meine holde Gänsemagd),

with which the hostess has little pa-
tience, and which sends her angrily into
the house.

Bourgeoisie
(39)

A waitress and the Stablemaid remain upon the scene; but the King's
Son is unconscious of their presence, as
he bewails his beggar's state and re-
solves to leave this ugly village and go
home again. Something reminds him of
the TORN WREATH (27), and, taking it
from his doublet, he breaks into the
lovely wreath song again, while a solo
violin sings of the GOOSE-GIRL (7), the
thought of whom gives him new courage. "Since I am born the son of a

Royalty (22)

king, I must make a king of myself"
(Bin ich als Königssohn geboren, zum
König muss ich mich selber machen),
he declares; and, swinging the wreath

Torn Wreath
(27)

high in the air, he goes into the inn just
as the townspeople begin to assemble.

Flutes and bagpipes are playing, the
villagers are singing their old FOLK-
DANCES (36), all, even the Stablemaid, are eager for the coming of the

Royalty (22)

King.

And yet, when the King's Son enters
the crowd again, and the host, in an-

swer to his appeal for work, engages
him as a swineherd, there is not one of
the multitude with vision clear enough
to recognize true Royalty as it stands
before them.

Folk-Dance (36) and Royalty (22) And so the dance goes on, the people, unmindful of the presence of the
King's Son, he almost equally unmindful of them, as he seats himself under
the LINDEN (6) to think of his fair
GOOSE-GIRL (7).

Again the sense of his dream comes
over him, this time with the picture of
the GOOSE-GIRL (7) definitely interwoven; and as he sits and ponders upon
it, we hear the lyrical EPISODE (42).

" From thy branches that o'er me
    darken,
Let on my brow the night dews fall,
Can I my vanished dream recall,
If in silence I hearken? "

(Lass die Nachtropfen deiner Zweige
Mir auf die Stirne niederrinnen.
Kann ich den Traum mir rücker-
    sinnen
Wenn ich lausche und schweige?)

Episode (42)

Lass die Nach - tro - pfen dei - ner

Zwei - ge mir auf die Stir - ne nie - der -

rin - nen, Kann ich den Traum mir rück-er - sin- nen

This is interrupted by the shouts of the Broommaker's thirteen children, who march in, singing and bringing with them an atmosphere of happy innocence.

Children's March (43)

Ambassadors (30)

Royal Children (8)

To them the Broommaker pompously reiterates the message that the King is due when the clock strikes twelve, and orders them to sing aloud their song:

" Who'll buy a broom,
A good King's broom,
Who'll buy a broom? "

(Wer kauft Besen,
Gute Königsbesen,
Gute Königsbesen?)

So their call is added, as the scene
rushes on, to the other sounds of rev-
elry, to the BOURGEOISIE (39) of the
host calling for one glass of unwatered
wine, to the DANCE MELODY (38) of
the people in the background.

One fair, sweet child goes to the
King's Son himself and offers to sell
him a broom. And, since she reminds
him of the maiden he loves, he allows
the child to persuade him to play with
her. She sings:

" Ring around the red rose bush,
Caught and torn my shirt is;
Little white goose bit my leg,
Oh, how bad the hurt is.
Bush shall no more roses carry,
Gander with a rod I'll harry,
Ring around the red rose bush—"

(Roter Ringelrosenbusch
Hat mein Hemd zerissen;
Weisses Schnabelgänslein hat
Mich in's Bein gebissen.
Busch darf nicht mehr Rosen tragen,
Weisses Gänslein werd ich schlagen.
Roter Ringelrosenbusch—)

But even before she finishes the game,
the playful mention of the ' little white

goose ' has sharpened the pain of his memories until he is overcome, and, putting his arms sadly around the child, he sits down again under the tree.

Then the noise of the FESTIVAL (35) wells up once more, with the rhythm of the FOLK-DANCE (36) always in evidence. It stops for a moment, as the people listen to the village elder and his memories of the good old days when the last King lived; then, continuing again, it ceases only when the Woodcutter is called upon to tell the story of their mission to the witch.

Regal State (23)

Festival (35)

More graphically than truly, he describes the horrors and dangers of the enchanted woods; the AMBASSADORS' (30) theme grows pompous and important in his long narration. But once he draws too largely upon his fancy, and the King's Son, who had passed them on their way, challenges the tale, speaking of their companion, the FIDDLER (33), and so verifying his story. The people are impatient of the interruption. " Hurry," shouts the chorus of voices, " tell us what she said " (Flink doch! Was hat sie gesagt?)

Death (18)

The orchestra combines the AMBAS-

SADORS (30) with the ROYAL CHIL-
DREN (8), as the Woodcutter answers:
" On the stroke of twelve, the King's
Son will appear " (Mit dem zwölften
Glockenton kommt der Königssohn).

Royalty (22) The elders swear that the Royal
Child shall have their kingdom. The
Ambassadors Woodcutter uses the enthusiasm of
(30) the occasion to embellish the story of
the way in which the King's Son may
be expected to arrive, and even the
children cry " Long live the King "
(Der König lebe hoch).
Then the King's son steps boldly
into the circle.

Royalty (22) " Could it then happen in no other
way?
Can a king not come in simpler
garb? "

(Könnt' es nicht anderer Weise ge-
schehn?
Kann ein König nicht kommen in
schlichtem Kleide?)

At once they are all in arms against
him; the Broommaker, the Innkeeper,
the Chorus, the Woodcutter, each press-
ing forward in turn to expound his own

view of royalty. The music of the passage is eloquent. With the first words of the King's Son, the motive of ROYALTY (22) appears and is maintained singly and alone through all that follows, repeated again and again, enlarged, developed, but always insisted upon, growing to its full height in the last attempt of the King's Son to make them see what true Royalty would be like, and then, failing of its purpose after all, and giving way to the motive of the FESTIVAL (35) and the vulgar INNKEEPER'S DAUGHTER (41), as she clamors for the King's Son to pay for what he had not ordered and could not eat.

Festival (35)

Royal
Children (8)

It is the spirit of the day that is in full swing when the first stroke of the clock brings sudden silence, followed by a wild rush for the gates. Only the King's Son stands still, fascinated by the sound of the bells which ring as in his dream, bringing back with them that forgotten vision of the Goose-Girl who is to come as Queen. The motives of BEAUTY (13) and of the ROYAL CHILDREN (8) combine and develop, until with the twelfth stroke the gates are opened and the Goose-Girl appears. Then, for the King's Son, everything fades out of sight but his own great love. " True! " (Wahr!), he exclaims; and the Love Motto (20) broadens out before us until it becomes more than a phrase, more than a melody, growing into the whole of the episode.

" Ardently longing, thus I have seen
You, oh my Queen, my noble Queen."

(Der ich mit Sehnen ergeben bin
O du meine hohe Königin.)

Quickly then it changes into a pathetic minor, as the people break into laughter at the thought of a Queen, barefoot, and with her geese behind her; and so the phrase is bandied about to the taunts of the populace. The King's Son rises to defend her:

Sword (21)
and Love
Motto (20)

" Let any one dare to touch the
Queen,
He shall know that a royal sword
is keen."

(Wag einer, die Königin zu berühren,
Soll er ein Königsschwert verspüren.)

The Fiddler, too, rushes in to save the people from the results of their own folly:

" You fools and dullards, are you so
    beguiled,
  Knows not one soul the Royal
    Child? "

(Ihr Narren, ihr Tölpel, seid ihr
    so blind,
  Erkennt nicht einer das Königs-
    kind?)

Fiddler as Apostle (34)

Love Motto (20)

With all the power of his own faith in their great destiny, the Fiddler pleads their ROYALTY (22); but only the child who has played with the King's Son looks up and listens.

" The feast is over " (Das Fest ist aus), cry the elders, and, jeeringly, the people ask, " And the Royal Children? " (Und die Königskinder?)

" Drive them out " (Die jagt hinaus), comes the answer; and again the LOVE MOTTO (20) in the minor, tells, better than words, of the sorrow in the hearts of the ROYAL CHILDREN (8) as they are driven from the gates, the crowd mocking and hooting at their heels.

Yet one who honors them is left behind to mourn their fate; and the curtain falls, not upon their own defeat, but upon the child, proclaiming still their ROYALTY (22).

Prelude to Act III

The Quest has failed. The King's
Son is a wanderer again, as he was
when he left his father's gates; but
without the hope that spurred him on,
and with the added weight of sorrow
for the beloved Goose-Girl who had
shared his failure.

The brilliance of the key of E Flat
is dulled to a minor to portray him so,
in the Introduction to the third act,
which heralds the denouement of the
opera, as the act itself reveals it. All
the added themes in this splendid prelude speak of the tragedy to come; the
motive of the Wasted Lives (44) of

**Wasted Lives
(44)**

the Royal Children; the poignant
Melody in B Flat Minor (45)—
sung by the oboe—which appears only
once again, but which, with its thrilling
renewal of the Love Motto (20), can-

**Melody in
B Flat Minor
(45)**

not be forgotten; above all, the fragment of the FIDDLER'S LAST SONG (46)
—derived from the motive, FIDDLER AS
APOSTLE (34)—which expresses all the
pain the world's nobler souls suffer from
the ignorance and cruelty and sordid-
ness of the sons of earth.

**Fiddler's Last
Song (46)**

Wo - hin bist du ge - gan - gen, O

Kö - nigs - toch-ter mein, in treu - er Lieb' um-

fan - - [gen vom trau - ten Buh - len dein?

ACT III

When the curtain opens, showing the
same scene as in the first act, but with
signs of winter and of ruin everywhere,
it is still in E Flat Minor that we hear
the motives of the LINDEN (6) and of
the GOOSE-GIRL (7), while from the
hut drifts the sound of a violin playing
strains reminiscent of the FIDDLER
(33). And when the Fiddler comes
out to feed the hungry doves, it is not
only of them he is thinking, but still of
the GOOSE-GIRL (7) and the YOUNG
PRINCE (24), as they seemed when the

Love Motto (20)

LINDEN (6) was in flower and their
love was young.

The voices of the Woodcutter and
the Broommaker, humbled though they
are into something quite different from
their old selves, bring with them no

Ambassadors Humbled (47)

sense of human companionship, such as
does the greeting of the Child:

" Fiddler, Fiddler, we're coming to
    you."

(Spielmann, Spielmann wir kommen
    zu dir.)

That, interrupted at first by the Fiddler himself, and then by the HUMBLED
AMBASSADORS (47), pleading their new
cause, begins again and grows into one
of those SONGS OF THE CHILDREN
(48), which nobody knows so well as
Humperdinck how to write, and which
sound as though they had grown out of
the very soil of Germany. Far back in
the first act, when the Goose-Girl re-
called her own childhood, a phrase from
this song crept naturally into the music.

Song of the Children (48)

Lie-ber Spielmann, al - le Kin-der und ich,   wir

ha - ben ge - be - ten, ge - fleht für dich.

Ambassadors Humbled (47)

Royal Children (8) (in Minor)

It is hard for the Fiddler to deny
the children's plea to go back with them
to Hellabrunn; but he has vowed never
to return, and it does not require the
Woodcutter's mention of the fatal
King's Day to strengthen his memories

of the causes that drove him forth.
Still the Child pleads, telling him that
she and her companions are firm in
their faith in the ROYALTY (22) of the
girl and the youth who came to them,
and all the other children echo her sen-
timents.

**Faith of the
Children (49)**

Führ' uns du, und wir zie - hen aus und
brin - gen die Kö - nigs - kin - der nach Haus.

Then the Fiddler lifts the Child in
his arms—glorying in the divine simplicity of youth—and, unable longer to
contain himself, he cries out against the
affliction which has rendered him unfit
to run alone through the world to seek
some clue to the Royal Children, hopelessly lost in the woods of winter.

The FIDDLER'S (33) motive is sub-
ordinated to a dramatic variant, and
both give way before ROYALTY (22) in
the Minor.

But the company of the children
brings new hope and thoughts of the
spring which must return, and we have
the musical sequence reversed—ROY-

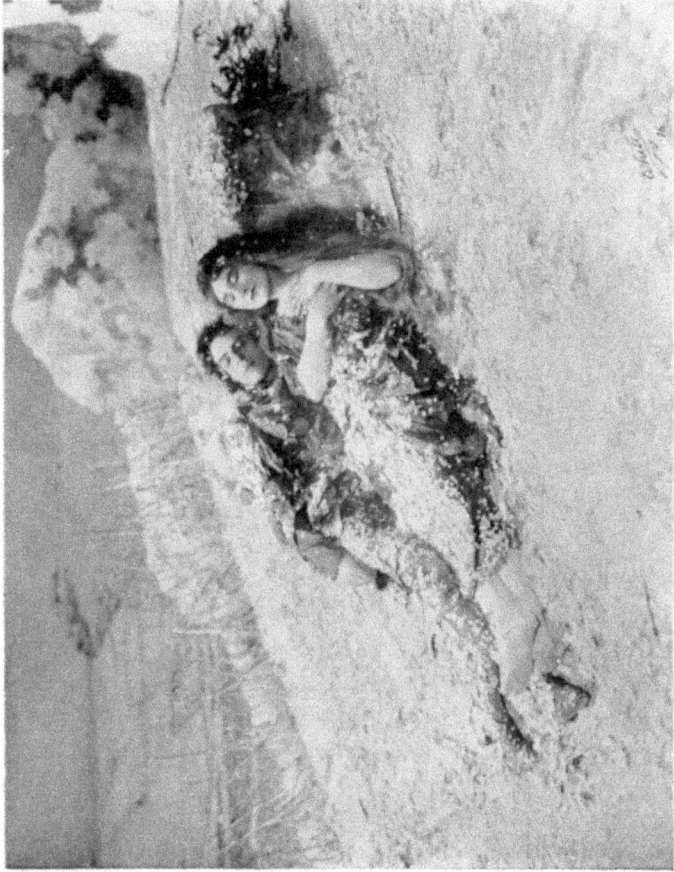

THE DEATH OF THE ROYAL CHILDREN

ALTY (22) in the Major, the variant of
the Fiddler, accounted for now as sig-
nifying his HOPE OF SPRING (50), the

**Hope of
Spring (50)**

FIDDLER (33) and the FAITH OF THE
CHILDREN (49), which he has come to
share before his speech ends:

" And we shall seek them and we
        shall find,
And songs we'll sing and wreaths
        we'll wind."

(Wir werden sie suchen und wer-
        den sie finden,
Und Lieder singen und Kränze
        winden.)

Fiddler (33)   Leaving the Ambassadors behind in
Ambassadors the hut, the Fiddler and his swarm of
Humbled (47) children go off into the woods, and
from the distance the breezes carry back
the melody of the FIDDLER'S LAST
SONG (46):

" Whither have you wandered,
    O royal maiden mine."

(Wohin bist du gegangen,
    O Königstochter mein.)

Longing (5)

The last words are drowned in a sudden gust; and then, after a moment's silence, there is a quick orchestral change to the motive of TRAGIC LOVE (51), as the King's Son descends the hillside, carrying the starving Goose-Girl in his arms.

Tragic Love (51)

Linden (6) and Goose-Girl (7)

The sight of the old place is to the girl like a renewal of her old self, but not one of unalloyed pleasure, since it carries with it the memory of the WITCHERY OF NATURE (11), which caused her such unhappiness.

Humbled Ambassadors (47)

Almost hopelessly, the King's Son goes to the door of the hut and knocks. The sound of the Woodcutter's voice in answer gives him courage to plead, with all the power of his TRAGIC LOVE (51), for "a bit of bread, a drop to drink" (Einen Bissen Brot, einen Tropfen Trank).

Even that is refused, and the GOOSE-

GIRL (7), in the Minor, draws him gently to the hillock, sighing, "We are beggars" (Wir sind Bettler). The motive of LONGING (5) starts, but breaks off quickly, succeeded by TRAGIC LOVE (51). Even beyond that, there is a depth of sorrow to be touched; and when the King's Son remembers that in this winter earth there is no longer any chance of finding food, the full consciousness of their WASTED LIVES (44) rushes in upon him.

What follows is but the pain and the pleasure that come to them from a memory of other days, sometimes clearly allied, as when the hope of a May to come brings up a picture of the other May, and the orchestra gives the WOOING (25), with FLIRTATION (4) and the QUEST (1); sometimes in quick transition, as when the King's Son recalls his adventures, and we have COQUETRY (40), FLIRTATION (4), WASTED LIVES (44), COQUETRY (40), FLIRTATION (4) and the LOVE MOTTO (20). The beautiful web now is tangled and torn; one motive seldom appears alone, seldom quite simply or complete. The DIVINE DISCONTENT

Wooing (25) (3) and the love that conquered it unite to say:

> " I saw you in danger and learned
>   to tremble."

> (Dir sah ich Gefahr und lernte
>   zittern.)

The LOVE MOTTO (20) blends into the REGAL STATE (23), in which they sat and sang, unmindful whether 'twere in sun or moonlight, in that time so different from this, where hunger and cold are pursuing, and DEATH (18), although disguised, confronts them.

Wasted Lives
(44)
and Love
Motto (20) Then, to show how little material suffering can affect her spirit, the Goose-Girl pulls off her sandals and dances before her lover.

> " Cometh my comrade from far-
>   away countries,
>   Passeth along like a bright sum-
>   mer's day,
>   Woven of silk is the doublet he
>   weareth,
>   Doublet of flax would too heav-
>   ily weigh."

(Kommt mein Geselle aus weiter
    Fremde,
Geht wie ein frischer Sommer
    daher.
Trägt er ein seidensponnenes
    Hemde,
Wär ihm ein linnen Hemde zu
    schwer.)

Goose-Girl's Dance (52)

Kommt mein Ge- sel - le aus Wei- - ter Fremde

And the dance is full of memories,
the LOVE MOTTO (20), ROYAL CHIL-
DREN (8), WASTED LIVES (44)—until
the silver SPINDLE (9) breaks and the
Goose-Girl falls exhausted. Does she
see the vision of DEATH (18) ap-
proaching as she wakens, crying

Magic Spell (17)

" Death cannot come, for I love
    you "

(Der Tod kann nicht kommen, Ich
    liebe dich) ?

And is a foreshadowing of the peace
of death already there, since we hear
a fragment of CONTENTMENT (26)
even as she says

" I will not die—my King is sad."

(Ich will nicht sterben—mein König
weint.)

The King's Son remembers his
CROWN (28); and, in spite of the
Goose-Girl's appeal,

Royalty (22)   " King, sell not your crown! "
and Love
Motto (20)
(König, verkauf deine Krone nicht!)

he knows that it is their only hope. He
has lost the path back to life; he has
sunk from ROYALTY (22) to become a
Death (18)   beggar.   As he breaks the crown, a
fragment of the motive of the YOUNG
PRINCE (24) appears to mock the
action.
The sacrifice is all in vain.   DEATH
(18) is upon them truly now, and the
motive, fully revealed, comes again and
again; first, when the Broommaker
shows his companion the old loaf he has
found; then, after the Woodcutter
Royalty (22)   has exchanged the chest for the crown,
and
Bourgeoisie   where he gives the loaf to the King's
(39)   Son; again, as the King's Son hands
the loaf to the maiden; again, as she

insists, " Not I alone, you too " (Nicht
ich allein, du auch).

Then the DEATH (18) changes to
the more specific motive of the POI-
SONED LOAF (15), which grows and develops as they eat, and then, as the
enchantment begins to work, gives way
to the WASTED LIVES (44). Yet, in
spite of the horror of the reality, the
pain of Death is hidden from them by
the very force of the magic; and suddenly the world of this life fades away
and leaves in their minds only the
thought of the WOOING (25) on the
day when the YOUNG PRINCE (24) was
in the first fresh CONTENTMENT (26)

Beauty (13) of his love, when he found the Goose-
Love Motto Girl tending her GEESE (10) as he
(20)
Goose-Girl (7) came over the mountains in QUEST (1)
of happiness.

The LOVE MOTTO (20) is nowhere
so rich and full as here, when, under
the Linden, they sink in a last embrace.
For the first time in the opera, they sing
together a duet, rich in CONTENTMENT
(26).

Love Motto " So let me kiss you and silent be,"
(20)

whispers the King's Son, as he dies.

Contentment (26) " So let me kiss you and silent be "

Divine Discontent (3) (Lass mich dich küssen und stille sein),

answers the Goose-Girl.

Poisoned Loaf (15) The poison is finishing its deadly work. Then, once again, with her last breath,

" Death cannot come for I love you "

(Der Tod kann nicht kommen, ich liebe dich),

sighs the Goose-Girl, dying with the thought of the YOUNG PRINCE (24) bringing CONTENTMENT (26) to her soul. And the work of the POISONED LOAF (15) is ended.

Bourgeoisie (39) and Royalty (22) Before the Fiddler and the Children come back from the woods, the falling snow has half-hidden the bodies of the Royal Children; and it needs the clue which the Woodcutter offers, when he shows the crown, to make the Fiddler suspect who the beggars were.

" Royal Children! Royal Children! " he calls, and when the dove leads the way to where they lie, he sinks down next to the dead bodies, bewailing bitterly the WASTED LIVES (44).

There follows the episode in which the other Children return, gazing curiously upon the scene, which is full of the atmosphere of the SPELL (17) and the sense of the WASTED LIVES (44). And the Fiddler, rising, tells, as best he can, the tragic tale. Here it is that the haunting MELODY IN B FLAT MINOR (45)—spoken of in the Prelude—appears again, melting into the LOVE MOTTO (20) and clouding it in pathos. Yet, in spite of his sorrow, the Fiddler is the first to feel the CONTENTMENT (26) with which the Young Prince and the Goose-Girl had met their death, united in love.

Royalty (22)

Love Motto (20)

So he gathers the Children about him, and they lift the bodies of the King's Son and the Goose-Girl on to the bier which he had made for himself. Then, singing again his noble song, the Fiddler heads the sad procession as it moves away.

Fiddler's Last Song (46)

From the distance, the fresh young voices are calling the Royal Children; but the motive of ROYALTY (22) is re-

versed and followed by the SPELL (17).
The Fiddler knows that they can not
return; knows, too, that the truth for
which they stood must not die with
them; and it is of the FIDDLER AS APOS-
TLE (34) that we hear as the opera
draws to a close.

Titles published by Travis & Emery:

Travis & Emery Music Bookshop
17 Cecil Court, London, WC2N 4EZ, United Kingdom. Tel. (+44) 20 7240 2129
© Travis & Emery 2009